WHEN WORDS COLLIDE:
A Crash Course in
Writing Poetry

A.L.S. Vossler

For Chel, Sara, and Lyn

Table of Contents

Foreword

This book about how to write poetry was the last work that A.L.S. Vossler ever completed. She began working on it in the last week of October 2018, finished writing in about 4 days, and edited it during November (while also participating in National Novel-Writing Month). She finished proofreading and formatting the book on Tuesday, December 4, and brought it to a local print shop that afternoon. The next day, Wednesday, December 5, 2018, A.L.S. Vossler lost her eleven-year battle with depression and bipolar disorder, despite all the best efforts of herself, her family, her counselor, and her doctors in keeping her safe. She took her own life around 6:30 that evening. Sadly, she never had a chance to see the finished version of *When Words Collide*, which has been so meaningful to her family and friends who have received copies since her untimely passing.

She was torn between a desire to add a bit to this book and publish it for Kindle, and an equal desire to sit on it and just give it as a Christmas present to those named on the dedication page. I have chosen to publish this book as is (although I have tried to improve its formatting), with the addition of this Foreword, as a tribute to my wife. This is the first of what I hope will be several posthumous works I publish for her, including a couple poetry collections she had started, as well as *Scylla*, the sequel to her first novel *Charybda* and finale of the *Worldstrait* series.

Somehow it seems fitting for A.L.S. Vossler's first posthumous work to be a poetry-writing guide aimed at new authors, combining both her love of poetry and her desire to help young authors, as shown in her first blog ("The Lonely Young Writer") and her love of tutoring.

It is my hope that those who read *When Words Collide* will find it useful as they write their own poetry.

- Chris Vossler, Husband and Executor of the Estate of A.L.S. Vossler

Chapter One: Introduction

What is Poetry?

"A poem should not mean / But be."
—Archibald MacLeish, "Ars Poetica"

There are a lot of fruity and elitist ideas out there about the definition of poetry. In his poem "Ars Poetica," Archibald MacLeish suggests that the purpose of a poem is to exist for its own sake, independent of any meaning. While this is a romanticized view of poetry, the truth of the matter is that the simplest definition of a poem is the same definition as all writing: a collection of words to which we assign meaning. Without *meaning*, there is not much point to writing in the first place — especially poetry, which in my opinion is essentially *meaning* condensed.

Now, I am not here to wax philosophical about the nature of poetry or present any ontological arguments about it. I had to deal with all of that in college and it was a snooze fest and a half. Rather, I am here to give you the skinny on how to write poetry. Unfortunately, this does bring us back to the question, "What is poetry?"

Poetry is, more or less, concise thought presented in an artful manner. It is words colliding on the page. That's it. Of course, the same could be said of prose. However, poetry does have distinct defining traits which separate it from prose, the most notable of which is that it is less wordy. Have no fear; if you think you cannot write poetry, let me assure you that if you can write prose, you can write poetry. Think of poetry as condensed prose presented with a little more flair. What flair is that? The flair of poetic devices.

Once you understand what poetic devices are, you can produce poetry just as artfully as you produce prose. The first, most complex, and most well known poetic device is that of structure. This encompasses such concepts as meter and rhyme—the sort of things that automatically come to mind when you hear the word "poetry." Another poetic device is the sound of the words themselves and what they contribute to the poem at large. There are many ways to use sound to enhance your poetry, such as alliteration, assonance, and consonance. Word choice and placement are key poetical devices as well, as each word must be carefully selected for the pithiest meaning, and then placed in a manner that draws attention to that meaning. Lastly, but certainly not least, are other poetic devices such as imagery, metaphor, repetition, the "turn," grammar, and even the shape of the poem. Not every poem will use all of these devices, but they are key weapons in your arsenal as you embark on your poetry writing journey. Near the end of this book I will demonstrate for you my simple five-step process for writing poetry, so you can see how at least one poet assembles words into a poem.

And now, it is time for you to turn the page and start down the path of your crash course in the art of making words collide.

Chapter Two: Structure

The Structure of Poetry

Poetry is unique among writing forms in that one of its defining traits is a specific structure of some kind. Even free verse, the least structured form of poetry of all, has a structure to it. The ways in which poetry can be structured vary wildly, but the main structures are metered verse, rhymed verse, pre-structured verse, and free verse. Obviously, the most prominent form of poetry is metered and rhymed verse, but as poetry has evolved, free verse has become more and more popular and pre-structured verse has fallen out of favor, relegated to classroom exercises. Nevertheless, whatever structure helps you to express your ideas and feelings best is the right structure for you.

Metered Verse

Meter is one way to bring music and cadence to your words, setting it apart from prose. Metered verse is, for some people, the most frustrating thing in the world. There is a lot of boring counting and strenuous thinking about where emphasis lands on syllables in words. It challenges you in a way that prose will not. At the same time, it can be one of the most rewarding forms simply because of how much work goes into it—and when you read it out loud, you will hear your words singing. Your metered poetry does not have to rhyme. The meter itself is enough of an art form to stand on its own merit.

So what is meter? Simply put, meter is the number of syllables and type of syllabic emphasis in a line of poetry. A metrical scheme is the format of meter throughout the entire work. The cool thing about meter is that you can totally make up your own metrical scheme for any given poem. In order to do that, it helps to know various types of metrical feet.

Metrical Feet

A metrical foot is the basic unit of meter. These are the four most common metrical feet:

Iamb (Iambic): da-DUM (a-WRY)
Trochee (Trochaic): DA-dum (NOR-way)
Dactyl (Dactylic): DA-dum-dum (STRAW-ber-ry)
Anapest (Anapestic): da-da-DUM (ab-so-LUTE)

Now, you've probably heard of iambic pentameter. Iambic pentameter is famous because it is what Shakespeare used. But what is it exactly? It is five (penta, as in pentagon) iambs in a single line of poetry. It does not necessarily mean five two-syllable words, because certain words are not stressed when we put them together—notably articles, demonstratives, pronouns, and so forth. So iambic pentameter would be this:

a-CROSS the SEA we SEE a FLY-ing BIRD

You may find that iambic is the easiest to write in meter. You can have as many feet in a line as you wish; it does not have to be five. It always pays off to experiment with writing poetry in different feet. For example, you can have dactylic trimeter (three):

BRIGHT-ly wrapped BUT-ter-scotch CAN-dies are

Or you could have trochaic tetrameter (four):

SWE-den HAS the FINE-st FISH there

You need not limit yourself to only one type of foot per line of poetry. You can have two iambs followed by a dactyl, for example, or a trochee followed by an anapest.

You can also create your own metrical scheme—four iambs in one line alternating with three iambs in the next could be one way to do it, or basically anything that strikes your fancy. As long as you are consistent, your poetry will have structure.

What if you have this gorgeous metrical scheme and find a word you really want to use, but it has the wrong number of syllables? Do what poets have done for centuries: ditch one of the syllables. You will see this all the time in Shakespeare and hymnody. The two-syllable "heaven" becomes a one-syllable "heav'n." You can also elide words together to ditch a syllable: "Many a" with three syllables can become "many'a" with only two. A missing syllable is denoted with an apostrophe.

The best part of meter? You do not even need to know the names of metrical feet. You can count out the number of syllables and decide where your accents will fall. If you start writing, listen with your inner ear for the cadence you have put in a line, and then duplicate it for the next line. Create a pattern. Let it flow.

Rhymed Verse

Perhaps even more than meter, we associate poetry with rhyme. Rhyme can be fixed in a rhyme scheme or can be used freely throughout a work. English is, unfortunately, one of the most rhyme-poor languages in the world, with a handful of words which have no true rhymes whatsoever. This means you may have to rely on *slant rhyme.* Slant rhyme is when you have word which sounds similar but is not a pure rhyme. Slant rhymes have *consonance,* i.e. the same ending consonant sound. You may also have two words which have *assonance,* i.e., the same vowel sound. (These will be discussed in more detail in the next chapter.) Both of these are acceptable ways to keep rhyme in your work without always being able to find that oh-so-perfect word.

Rhymed poetry does not have to be metered — rhyme is enough of an art form to stand on its own merits.

Rhyme Schemes

Rhyme schemes can basically be whatever you want them to be. If you are writing in *stanzas* (a way of dividing poetry into numbers of lines), you will assign specific lines to rhyme. In a four-line stanza (*quatrain*), which is the most common for some reason, this may look like ABAC (where each letter represents the ending rhyme), or it may look like ABCB. You can also choose ABCC. Or AABC. Or, if you like a real challenge, you can give each line a different rhyme, but the next stanza must have exactly the same rhyme per line as the preceding: ABCD, ABCD, etc. The rules are whatever you choose them to be. Whatever you choose, make it consistent—or your poetry will cease to have a rhyme scheme. A common occurrence in poetry is a *rhymed couplet:* two lines with the same meter which rhyme with each other. Rhymed couplets stand out greatly in any rhyme scheme, so be sure that they are beautiful or poignant for the greatest effect.

Free Rhyme

You may be wondering how rhyme can be effective at all without a fixed format. Well, let me assure you that it most definitely can. Read the following excerpt of Christina Rossetti's "Goblin Market", an exciting narrative poem. There is no fixed rhyme scheme to discern, but there is a heavy reliance on rhyme words.

> Morning and evening
> Maids heard the goblins cry
> "Come buy our orchard fruits,
> Come buy, come buy:
> Apples and quinces,
> Lemons and oranges,
> Plump unpecked cherries,
> Melons and raspberries,
> Bloom-down-cheeked peaches,
> Swart-headed mulberries,
> Wild free-born cranberries,
> Crab-apples, dewberries,
> Pine-apples, blackberries,
> Apricots, strawberries; —
> All ripe together

In summer weather, —
Morns that pass by,
Fair eves that fly;
Come buy, come buy:
Our grapes fresh from the vine,
Pomegranates full and fine,
Dates and sharp bullaces,
Rare pears and greengages,
Damsons and bilberries,
Taste them and try:
Currants and gooseberries,
Bright-fire-like barberries,
Figs to fill your mouth,
Citrons from the South,
Sweet to tongue and sound to eye;
Come buy, come buy." (1-31)

Notice that rather than using a fixed rhyme scheme, Rossetti uses a lot of repeated rhymes, especially with anything rhyming with "berries." Also note the repeated use of words that rhyme with "buy." Some lines do not even have a rhyming line, and simply stand out on their own. Even without a fixed meter, the poetry has a lilt and music to it because of the places where Rossetti chooses to rhyme.

So how do you achieve something as glorious as that? It is not an easy feat, but it can be done. Repetition is your friend here, as Rossetti demonstrates. Another friend is your intuition. Free rhyme is just that—free, so if you try to bring any kind of logic to it, you will develop a rhyme scheme. Rhyme based on *feeling*. Does it *feel* right to have a certain pair of words rhyme? Do it. Do you want to draw attention to certain lines? Rhyme them. A rhymed couplet stands out like a beacon in a poem with no fixed rhyme structure.

You can create an unstructured type of music with your free rhyme, but it requires a high degree of intuition. If you don't trust your intuition, then free rhyme is not for you. The more poetry you write (and read), the more willing you may be to experiment with such techniques as free rhyme.

Pre-structured Verse

There are a variety of pre-structured forms of verse that have been in use for a long time. Some of the most popular forms are the acrostic, haiku, blank verse, and the sonnet. While these have largely been pigeonholed into classroom exercises, beginning poets may like them for the safety of having parameters laid out.

The Acrostic

The acrostic is a poem which dates back to some of the earliest poetry on record: the Psalms. It relies not on rhyme or meter for structure, but rather draws its structure from the alphabet. The first line begins with 'A,' the second with 'B,' the third with 'C,' and so on. Obviously, the Psalms follow the Hebrew alphabet. For an example, look at Psalm 119, which is labeled in subsections such as "aleph," "beth," or "daleth." That is because Psalm

119 is an acrostic; every line of the first section begins with "aleph."

A modern variation on the acrostic is to take a phrase or word and use the same process, but with the order of the letters in the phrase rather than the alphabet.

The goal is still to be artful and poetic, making use of beautiful words and powerful imagery, but you have the added challenge of starting each line with a specific letter.

Haiku

The haiku is a widely known Japanese form of poetry. It is a three line, un-rhymed, un-metered poem with five syllables in the first and third lines and seven syllables in the second line. It is deceptively easy to write, and difficult to master. Because you are working in such a tiny amount of space, you must pack as much meaning into those seventeen syllables as you possibly can. Word choice is paramount. The goal of the haiku is to present a single thought or moment in time, fitting in with the Japanese concept of impermanence. Metaphor is often heavily utilized to present comparisons without cluttering up the poem with "like" or "as," each of which is a costly syllable. Avoid also articles and demonstratives, if at all possible. Make it as pithy as possible. Write on any topic you want; there is no such thing as a wrong topic when it comes to haiku. You are just trying to capture that single thought or moment. Don't make it too complicated.

Blank Verse

Blank verse is un-rhymed iambic pentameter. It is what all of Shakespeare's plays are written in. It's a good way to practice your meter-writing skills without having to worry about rhyme. Like haiku, and all poetry for that matter, it can be about whatever you want it to be. You may divide it into stanzas or not. Simply focus on the meter.

The Sonnet

The sonnet is perhaps the most well-known pre-structured verse in Western literature, owing to its origins in Italy and its popularity in England. All sonnets are in iambic pentameter and are fourteen lines long. The Shakespearean and Spenserian both end with a *heroic couplet*. A heroic couplet is two lines in iambic pentameter which rhyme. Writing sonnets can be rewarding and fun. Almost everyone had to write one for high school English at some point, but it has purpose well beyond a simple exercise. Like haiku, you are limited to a certain amount of space, so pith is vital. Pick only the choicest, most powerful words.

Shakespearean (English)

The Shakespearean Sonnet, also known as the English sonnet, consists of three quatrains (sets of four lines) and one couplet. The rhyme scheme is as follows:

ABAB CDCD EFEF GG

Spenserian

The Spenserian sonnet was developed by Edmund Spenser. It also consists of three quatrains and a couplet. The rhyme scheme is as follows:

ABAB BCBC CDCD EE

Petrarchan (Italian)

The Petrarchan sonnet was developed by the Italian poet Petrarch. It consists of an *octave* (eight lines) and a *sestet* (six lines) and uses the following rhyme scheme:

ADDAABBA CDCDCD (or the final sestet may also be CDEEDE)

Free Verse

Ah, free verse. The most confusing form of poetry there is, because there is no definitive structure. Punctuation need not apply. There is no rhyme, there is no meter, and there are no rules.

Well, no rules except for the rules, of course.

Why Free Verse?

So, why free verse? What is its purpose? If it has none of the qualities of the structures mentioned heretofore, how is it any different than prose? It is merely prose split into lines?

No. No, it is not.

Like other forms of poetry, it is less wordy and pithier than prose. It makes a much heavier use of metaphor than prose does, and makes use of the natural cadence and sound of words to be musical rather than cramming them into meter or forcing rhyme. It uses the power of word choice and strong words to make it artful. It is everything good prose is, but condensed and made more powerful, more musical, more metaphysical, more *everything*.

The "Structure" of Free Verse

Believe it or not, free verse is not truly without structure. What structure is that? Whatever structure you choose. You may choose to use stanzas or not. They can be even stanzas or uneven stanzas. They need not be consistent for the entire poem, either. "The Second Coming" by W.B. Yeats, for example, is broken into uneven stanzas. The challenge with free verse is that every stanza break is significant. A stanza break represents a shifting of topic, or a progression of story, or a signal of the poetic "turn" taking place (more on that later). A single line is intended to call attention to itself, suggesting it has a meaning the author wishes his or her audience to take particular note of. Sometimes it is used purely for dramatic effect.

Where you break the lines also matters, which you will learn more about in Chapter 4, "Word Choice and Placement." Sometimes a line will run on and on until it is appropriate to break it; other times a line will be little more than one or two words. This sounds like utter chaos, but there is logic to it: lines are broken thematically, just as stanzas are broken thematically. It's *controlled* chaos.

While there is no meter in free verse, there can be cadence. It is simply an irregular cadence. Typically you find that from line to line there is not a match, but each line has its own rhythm. This rhythm is produced by choosing words which have a lot of similar sounds (such as "Turning and turning in the widening gyre" from Yeats' "The Second Coming") in them. It can be achieved from line to line with repetition of phrases or phrase structure.

Free verse is not for everyone. Some people find it difficult to wrap their minds around. Others find that it is the only kind of poetry they like. The best way to understand free verse is to read a lot of it, and it is also the best way to learn how to write it. If you read enough, you begin to see the patterns that emerge.

Why Structure Matters

Structure is one of the main defining characteristics of poetry. Without structure of *some* kind, even the chaotic structure of free verse, poetry becomes nothing more than pretty prose. Whether you use meter, rhyme, a pre-determined structure, or free verse, your poem needs structure to bring it to life.

Chapter Three: Sound

Why Sound Matters

Poetry is one type of literature which is meant to be enjoyed aloud, making sound another of its crucial defining characteristics. It is also one of the easiest ways to bring a musical feel to your poetry; hard consonants become percussion, and long vowel sounds become song. Repeated sounds create a rhythm where there would otherwise be none. Most important of all, how something audibly sounds affects the meaning as well. If a poem is about a lovely topic but is full of harsh, guttural sounds and hard sharp consonants, it can suggest a sinister layer of meaning to the poem. Likewise, a poem about an ugly topic made lyrical and beautiful sounding may suggest that there is beauty in all things, even those we may not find conventionally attractive.

Types of Sound in Poetry

Poetry relies on a variety of types of sound to create a pleasing auditory experience. The most common, of course, is rhyme at the end of lines, but there are other tools to choose from, such as alliteration, assonance, consonance, internal rhyme, and words which mimic other sounds.

Alliteration

Alliteration is when two or more words begin with the same consonant or consonant blend. For example, the phrase "breakfast bread" has alliteration in it. Alliterative words can create a pattern or rhythm in your work. You may have been told to avoid alliteration in prose, and this is sound advice, as it may come across as pretentious and/or awkward. In poetry, however, it is a vital tool. It can be overused, certainly. Too much alliteration can be comical, which is perfect if you are trying to be funny. (By too much alliteration, I mean having it for every word in a line.) At the same time, if you are not, you may want to dial your use of it back.

Assonance

Assonance is when two words contain the same vowel sounds but not the same consonant sounds. "Ground" and "cow" have assonance with each other. Like alliteration, it is great for bringing a cadence to your work if you are writing free verse, or emphasizing your established cadence if you are writing with meter.

Consonance

Consonance is when words end in the same consonants or consonant blends. "Pants" and "hunts" have consonance. These words may sound like they are rhymed, but because they do not have the same vowel sound in addition to the consonants, it is not a pure rhyme but a slant rhyme. Hard consonants like 'k,' 'd,' and 'ch' create a punctuated feel in poetry, almost like tapping a snare, while soft consonants like 's,' 'l,' and 'n' create a more legato feel, like the smooth changes from tone to tone with a French horn.

Internal Rhyme

Internal rhyme is extra fun, in my opinion. It is when you have two rhyming words within the same line. You can achieve a similar effect by using assonance or consonance (slant rhyme). It may also span two lines, where a word inside one line (not the ending word) rhymes with another word inside the next line (also not the ending word). The effect this achieves is one of added urgency or emphasis

Words that Mimic Other Sounds

One of the most effective ways to utilize sound in poetry is to use words which mimic other sounds. I'm not speaking strictly of *echoic* words (also called *onomatopoeic* words: words which are intended to imitate real-life sounds, like "bark" for the sound a dog makes) here, but words whose consonants or vowels are reminiscent of other sounds. A great example of this is in Robert Hayden's "Those Winter Sundays."

> Sundays too my father got up early
> and put his clothes on in the blueblack cold,
> then with cracked hands that ached
> from labor in the weekday weather made
> banked fires blaze. No one ever thanked him.
>   (1-5)

The use of hard 'k' sounds so frequently mimics the sound of ice cracking. Another good one is Richard Snyder's "A Mongoloid Child Handling Shells on the Beach," which uses frequent sibilant consonants (s, z, sh, zh) to suggest the rushing of ocean waves:

> She turns them over in her slow hands,
> as did the sea sending them to her;
> broken bits from the mazarine maze,
> they are the calmest things on this sand.(1-4)

You may certainly also use echoic words to great effect. The reasoning behind this is a little more obvious. It helps by creating an auditory experience for your reader. "Loud" echoic words, such as in the phrase "Wham! Bam! The door does slam," create immediate tension, whereas gentle echoic words, such as "I mew, and purr, and meow so soft" create a sense of peace and relaxation (notice also how the alliterative sibilance of "so soft" adds to the effect). You can lure your reader into this relaxed type of sound, only to switch to something harsh and startling, like a jump scare in a movie. Obviously you would only do this if it is your intent—but it can show a dramatic shift in the tone of the poem.

The Art of Sound in Poetry

Utilizing sound in poetry requires an awareness of the words you are using as well as a degree of creativity and imagination. The tools of alliteration, assonance, consonance, internal rhyme, and words that mimic other words will take you far in making your poetry sound gorgeous.

Chapter Four: Word Choice and Placement

Why Word Choice and Placement Matter

Poetry is like a container for ideas—a suitcase, if you will. When you are packing a suitcase for a trip, you need to consider carefully which items you will bring with you on your journey. It would not do well to pack only t-shirts and shorts when going to Maine in the fall, nor would it be wise to pack sweaters and thick, woolen socks for visiting Texas in the summer. The placement of items in your suitcase is also important. For example, you might like your toiletries near the top for easy removal when going through airport security, or you might like to put heavy items such as shoes near the bottom so your suitcase is not top-heavy. Each word in your poem is like an item going into the suitcase for your poetic journey. You must choose only those words which suit the poem's needs, and you must place them in such a fashion that creates a maximum poetic effect.

Word Choice

Much like packing a suitcase, poetry requires fitting as much information into as tight a space as possible, so you must choose words which convey as much information as possible. When choosing words, select ones that are rich in connotations. As you may already be aware, a word's denotation is its literal meaning, while connotation is the implied meaning.

This does not necessarily mean that you must choose long or complicated words, but be sure that they mean exactly what you are trying to say. If you have to beef up the one word you have chosen with a lot of other words to find the desired effect, then try to find a single word which will convey the same meaning. For example, "the repeated sound of bells" could be replaced with the word "tintinnabulation." Notice that you are not necessarily trimming syllables in this case, but you are choosing something which sounds more interesting. This brings us to another element of word choice: consider how the word you are choosing sounds. While "honey-like" would work in its conciseness, consider choosing a word which means the same thing, but sounds more beautiful: "mellifluous." Both "tintinnabulation" and "mellifluous" are interesting sounding— particularly the former, which has a repeated syllable.

Consider using more unique words for simple ones, like colors—"cerulean" or "azure" for blue, for example, or "jet" or "ebon" for black, "verdant" for green, or "vermilion" for red. Do not feel like you have to choose the "fancier" word all the time. However, if you want to say "blue" but need four syllables, then "cerulean" is perfect for you. Pay attention to the sounds, though—the simpler words may serve you better depending on what effect you are trying to achieve in your poem.

A great way to increase your poetic vocabulary is to scour your dictionary for interesting-sounding words. If this sounds like the most boring thing there is, sign up for word-of-the-day emails from any number of reputed dictionary websites. All the same, reading through the dictionary offers a lot more discovery value. Read the dictionary for say, five minutes a day or so, and write down any words which stand out to you (be sure to make note of their meaning, because if you're like me, you will forget what they mean after fifteen minutes).

Sometimes a word itself is enough to inspire an entire poem, so this is a great way to get your creative juices flowing.

Word Placement

Once you have picked the perfect words for your poem, you need to be mindful of where you are placing them. If you are writing with meter, the meter will most likely dictate your word placement for you. A general rule of thumb is to avoid ending lines with "weak" words like articles and demonstratives. Verbs, nouns, and adjectives are the strongest words with which to end a line. If at all possible, begin lines with strong words as well. I am by no means saying that articles and demonstratives are to be shunned entirely, but if you can get by without them, then do so. Sometimes you will need them for the poem to make sense. Sometimes you will need them to fill a metrical foot. The idea is to use them sparingly.

Word placement is especially key in free verse, as the placement of words within lines as well as the poem at large can greatly affect the sound or improvised lilt of the work. Ending lines in weak words will suck the life from your free verse poem and make it limp and ineffective. If you must break a line (for aesthetic purposes, for example) then you should begin your next line with the weak word rather than ending a line with it. This is because the last word of a line sticks in the mind of the reader more than the first word does.

Pack Poetry like a Suitcase

Word choice and placement can make or break a poem in the same way that packing for a trip can make or break your vacation. Just like you would not pack a coat when a t-shirt will do, do not use a complex word when a simple one will serve you just as well; likewise, do not string together lots of simple words when a single complex one will communicate the same thing. Strong words make for strong poetry, while weak words make for weak poetry. Since weak words are not always avoidable, placing them in such a manner that they are not as noticeable makes for a stronger poem. By being mindful of the contents of your suitcase, you can have a great vacation—by being mindful of your words and where you put them, you can write great poetry.

Chapter Five: Other Poetic Devices

Why Other Poetic Devices Matter

While poetry is defined heavily by structure, sound, and word choice and placement, there are other poetic devices that make poetry what it is. Not all of them must be used at the same time, but they are key in writing a strong poem. Repetition adds a musical feel. Metaphor makes for rich, meaning-packed poetry. A "turn" adds a surprise element to your work. Imagery paints beautiful pictures. Grammar, or lack thereof, can change the meaning of your poem altogether. Lastly, shape, while the least common of poetic devices, adds an extra dimension to your work.

Repetition

Repetition is used heavily in some of the oldest poetry on record: the Psalms. The Hebrews made effective use of it in their poetry and other literature. If you sit down and read a few psalms, you will come across several occasions of repetition. One of my favorite examples is from Psalm 130:5-6:

> I wait for the LORD, my soul waits,
> and in his word I hope;
> my soul waits for the LORD
> more than watchmen for the morning,
> more than watchmen for the morning.
> (English Standard Version)

Notice the repetition of "my soul waits" and "more than watchmen for the morning." Despite this poem having no rhyme or meter in English, the words have a musical quality to them. The repetition also represents the absolute longing the poet feels for the Lord's aid, creating powerful emotions in the reader.

Repetition has not fallen out of use since the days of the Psalms. It is used to great effect in almost every era of literature.

Another great example of a poem with repetition in it is Alfred Noyes' "The Highwayman." It is a perfect example of poetry, and I will use it to show every poetic device in this chapter except for shape. I highly recommend you read it. From the very first stanza, we see an example of repetition:

> The wind was a torrent of darkness among the
> gusty trees.
> The moon was a ghostly galleon tossed upon
> cloudy seas.
> The road was a ribbon of moonlight over the
> purple moor,
> And the highwayman came riding—
>   Riding—riding—

The highwayman came riding, up to the old inn-door. (1-6)

The cadence of the word "riding" and its repetition mimics the clip-clop of horse's hooves. But this is not the only example in this poem. In fact, almost every stanza contains some case of repeated words, particularly in the last two lines. Noyes also repeats the imagery of the moon and the road in multiple cases. The final two stanzas are almost word-for-word the same as the first and third. If you read the whole poem, you can see how musical it is, between the lilt of its meter and the repetition of words in just the right places.

Repetition vs. Redundancy

You may have been told to avoid repetition because it is redundant. In prose, it can become a problem to have the same words used over and over. But as you can see from "The Highwayman," it's an important poetic device. How can you tell, then, when you have ceased using the device effectively and have slipped into simple redundancy? For one thing, if your repetition does not create a pattern or a lilt, then it has little virtue and you should discard it. For another, if the repetition is of a line that has little emotional weight or does not sound interesting, it might not be worth repeating in the first place. Repetition adds emphasis and focus to an important word, phrase, line, or concept Finally, trust your intuition. If you feel you may have overdone it on the repetition, try something else.

Metaphor

You may be familiar with the definition of metaphor as "a comparison without using 'like' or 'as.'" In poetry, it is used heavily. Simile is also used, but "like" and "as" are costly in a situation where every syllable counts. Instead of using "like" or "as" to compare, a metaphor takes one concept and says that it *is* another concept. Like repetition, it appears in the Psalms also, such as in Psalm 18:10a: "The name of the LORD is a strong tower." Psalm 46:11 likewise says, "The God of Jacob is our fortress."

"The Highwayman," as another one of its splendid qualities, is replete with metaphor. The first three lines alone are nothing but metaphor:

> The wind was a torrent of darkness among the
> gusty trees.
> The moon was a ghostly galleon tossed upon
> cloudy seas.
> The road was a ribbon of moonlight over the
> purple moor… (1-3)

In other places in the poem, Noyes says "His eyes were hollows of madness" (line 20) and "the road was a gypsy's ribbon looping the purple moor" (line 39). In another place he uses another literary device much like a metaphor to describe the sound of gunfire disrupting the night: "Her musket shattered the moonlight" (line 77). This is not a direct comparison. Rather, it uses "shattered" as a stand-in for "the disruptive sound of a gunshot" and "moonlight" for "the peacefulness of the night." This is known as *metonymy*, a figure of speech where one concept stands for another.

Metaphor is an important tool in poetry, even more so than simile. Prose is often more literal, while poetry is more figurative. What better way to achieve that than with metaphor or metonymy?

Imagery

Imagery is a simple concept which can be difficult to master. It is the art of painting a picture with words. Noyes gives us a perfect example of imagery in his description of the highwayman.

> He'd a French cocked-hat on his forehead, a bunch of lace at his chin,
> A coat of the claret velvet, and breeches of brown doe-skin.
> They fitted with never a wrinkle. His boots were up to the thigh.
> And he rode with a jewelled twinkle,

His pistol butts a-twinkle,
His rapier hilt a-twinkle, under the jewelled
sky. (7-12)

Metaphor can also be used to create imagery, as in the first stanza of "The Highwayman." Note how Noyes sets the scene using nothing but metaphor in the first three lines. They say "A picture is worth a thousand words," but note how few words it takes to immediately paint a perfect picture of the setting and the character. It takes only twelve lines of poetry, and we don't even need a picture drawn for us. The words accomplish it beautifully.

The "Turn"

The "turn" is when a poem takes, as you might guess, an unexpected turn. It is most commonly associated with the sonnet, where the last two lines are often a shift in thought. For example, in Shakespeare's Sonnet 130 ("My mistress' eyes are nothing like the sun") he spends the whole sonnet talking about how his mistress is not as fair as any of these grandiose conceits (a conceit is an exaggerated comparison) that were so common in love poetry at the time. But he concludes with this:

> And yet, by heaven, I think my love as rare
> As any she belied with false compare. (13-14)

Essentially, he is saying his love is every bit as valid as the love of those who write in conceits, if not more so. This is taking the concept of the poem (my mistress isn't that pretty) and turning it on its head (but my love is pure because I am not falsely comparing her to other things).

Noyes also has an unexpected turn in "The Highwayman." If you have not gone and read the poem yet, be aware that I am about to drop some serious spoilers. In the end, both the highwayman and his lover Bess are killed. This seems to be the end of the poem. Yet the final two stanzas depict them repeating their actions from the first part of the poem:

And still of a winter's night, they say, when the
    wind is in the trees,
When the moon is a ghostly galleon tossed
    upon cloudy seas,
When the road is a ribbon of moonlight over
    the purple moor,
A highwayman comes riding—
      Riding—riding—
A highwayman comes riding, up to the old inn-
    door.

Over the cobbles he clatters and clangs in the
    dark inn-yard.
He taps with his whip on the shutters, but all is
    locked and barred.
He whistles a tune to the window, and who
    should be waiting there
But the landlord's black-eyed daughter,
      Bess, the landlord's daughter,
Plaiting a dark red love-knot into her long black
    hair. (90-102, emphasis original)

The turn is sudden and sharp. This poem isn't
just a narrative poem about a highwayman and his
lover; it's a ghost story. It's not just about the nature
of sacrificial love; it's a promise that love goes on

after death. So you see that the turn is not necessarily a contradiction of the poem preceding, but a shift in thought or a surprise twist.

Grammar in Poetry

Grammar is an important aspect of poetry. It is important to write out your thoughts using proper English syntax and punctuation. It is also important that you not use proper English syntax and punctuation in your poetry.

Allow me to clarify. Once you have decided whether or not you are going to use proper English syntax and punctuation in your poetry, then proceed with your plans.

Whether or not you use proper grammar can have a great effect on your poem. Stream-of-consciousness poetry is best left free and without punctuation—just bear in mind that if you do use punctuation in a largely unpunctuated poem, it draws huge attention to the line with the period at the end. If you are writing a narrative poem, it is a good idea to use proper syntax and punctuation, just as "The Highwayman" does. However, you can still get away with not using any real grammar in a narrative poem, as E.E. Cummings does in his poem "Anyone Lived in a Pretty How Town":

> anyone lived in a pretty how town
> (with up so floating many bells down)
> spring summer autumn winter
> he sang his didn't he danced his did (1-4)

Notice how there is not any capitalization or necessarily proper syntax in this stanza. Think about how different it would be if you added those. It would convey entirely different meaning. In fact, the whole poem would be different—it would be in serious danger of making sense. Okay, that was a joke. The poem makes sense if you read it enough, but on first glance, *wow*, it is hard to read.

Speaking of capitalization, it is customary to capitalize every line of poetry. However, you may choose to follow prose capitalization rules, where only the words which begin sentences or are proper are capitalized.

The important rule is to choose what you are going to do, and then stick with it.

Shape

Shape is the last, and perhaps least commonly used, poetic device I will discuss. It is a fairly old concept, but is not seen very often. It is when the words on the page create a shape. One of the most famous shape poems is George Herbert's 1633 poem "Easter Wings," which was originally printed sideways so the words would suggest the shape of angel wings:

Lord, who createdst man in wealth and store,
　　Though foolishly he lost the same,
　　　　Decaying more and more,
　　　　　Till he became
　　　　　　Most poore:
　　　　　With thee
　　　　　O let me rise
　　　As larks, harmoniously,
　　And sing this day thy victories:
Then shall the fall further the flight in me.

My tender age in sorrow did beginne
　　And still with sicknesses and shame.
　　　　Thou didst so punish sinne,
　　　　　That I became
　　　　　　Most thinne.
　　　　　With thee
　　　　Let me combine,
　　　And feel thy victorie:
　　For, if I imp my wing on thine,
Affliction shall advance the flight in me.

Writing in shape can be a fun and challenging
way to write poetry, making it a visual as well as
auditory experience.

A World of Options

As you can see, there are a variety of poetic devices at your disposal when writing a poem. You can use as many or as few of them as you see fit, but the more you use, the richer your poem will be.

Chapter Six: Building a Poem

The Five-Step Process

Everybody writes poetry differently, but I will present you with the five-step process that works best for me, and I hope it will be useful to you as well. I *highly* recommend writing your poetry in longhand. Once it's finished, you can type it up and make revisions as you see fit, but the act of putting pen to paper will help you to be more creative. I will demonstrate the building of a poem in this section. First, you begin by choosing a topic. Then, you come up with word associations. Choosing a structure is the next step, and then you begin crafting the poem. Finally, you revise your work.

The most important rule to remember when writing poetry is not to stress yourself out—not every poem will be a gold mine, but even the ones that aren't are still good practice.

And, like any other discipline, the only way you'll get better is with practice.

Step 1: Choose a Topic

Choosing a topic can be difficult to do. With so many things to write about, how can you even pick one? There are a few ways to come up with ideas. A random title generator may spark some inspiration, or a writing prompt can help you out. Is there a feeling or problem that's been building up inside you? Write about that. Once your topic is chosen, spend some time pondering it before you put pen to page. The topic I chose for my demonstration is "a storm," provided by a helpful book of prompts entitled *Write the Poem*, published by Piccadilly. I conjure up an image of the storms building on the plains of the Midwest, watching the clouds build higher and higher as lightning leaps from cloud to cloud.

Step 2: Word Associations

The next thing I do after choosing a topic and pondering it for a few minutes is come up with word associations. I write down all the words that come to mind when I think of my topic—even the ones that aren't seemingly related. I try to choose words that are packed with meaning or are beautiful sounding. I will sometimes pull out a thesaurus for more inspiration. I incorporate those words into phrases and see which ones I like. My book of prompts has some ideas, but I don't like all of them. Instead, the first thing that comes to mind is "raindrops." Admittedly, that's kind of boring, but I jot it down anyway. Then I think of one of my mother's favorite phrases: "The sky is heavy." A few of the words in the prompt book stick with me, such as "roaring,", "raging," "tempestuous," "blast," "gale," and "wrath." Other words and phrases come to mind, like "roiling clouds" and "burgeoning." Once I have a collection of inspiring words and phrases, I move on to the next step.

Step 3: Choose a Structure

The next step is to choose a structure. Do you want to write something metered and rhymed? Decide ahead of time what you are going to do so you can do it from the beginning. You may find that halfway through you want to change your structure. Free verse may easily become metered, or metered verse may turn into free verse. Let that shift happen if it does, and don't worry about changing anything until step five. Choose a structure that suits your topic—stories lend themselves well to meter and rhyme, while poems about feelings or fleeting thoughts may be better suited to free verse. Bear in mind that some meters and rhyme schemes sound like Doctor Seuss, so unless your goal is to be satirical, avoid this. For my poem about a storm, I decided to go with free verse, since I feel that a) a demonstration of the ever-confusing free verse would be helpful to my readers, and b) it is simply what "felt" right for the topic. After all, storms have no discipline—they are wild and unpredictable, and free verse lends itself to that notion.

Step 4: Begin Crafting

Once you have chosen the structure you are going to follow, it's time to begin crafting your poem. Writing a poem can take anywhere from a few minutes to days to months. It depends on how much you are able to work on at a time, and what your own personal creative process is like. You may find yourself immediately disliking something you have written. Cross it out, but leave it legible in case you want to come back to it. Use the words you found to be inspiring, and try to feature them prominently. You may, as I often do, cross everything out and start over with a new structure altogether. The most important thing here is to be flexible and patient with yourself, or you'll never finish a single poem. As you write, remember all the poetic devices at your disposal and make use of them as you see fit.

I begin by penning a few words:

Raindrops fall.
Gentle, they fall, at first.
Wind, once soft, now howls.
Raindrops pelt.
And

At this point, I decide I do not like the way this is written, but I like the direction it is taking me. The idea of the storm building slowly resonates with me. So I cross out everything and try something else:

Pattering rain

I immediately cross this out. While storms sometimes begin gently, I am thinking of a huge Nebraska storm here, the kind that turns the sky black and immediately begins pelting rain at painful speeds. Then my mother's phrase of "The sky is heavy" comes to mind. I decide to use that to open the poem:

The sky is heavy.

This feels good because of its use of metaphor. Obviously, the sky itself has no weight, but it becomes a stand-in concept for the gallons and gallons of rain and pounds upon pounds of hail waiting in those clouds which are in the sky. Next, I write:

Black clouds billow,
Burdened with weight.

This carries over the concept of the sky being heavy, as well as the blackness of the clouds built like a huge puff of ash being blasted from a smithing billows. Notice I choose a near-alliterative pair of words, "black" and "billow," and then carry over from "billow" into "burden" in the next line. Also, "black clouds" has two hard 'k' sounds next to each other, which can be reminiscent of the crack of lightning. Not sure how to move forward, I go back to some of my associative words. "Wrath" comes to mind:

> Lightning's wrath
> In thunderclaps

Notice the assonance between the words "wrath" and "claps," which create a near rhyme that draws attention to this particular part of the poem I'm writing. I chose to do this because thunder is loud and attention-getting, too. I then think of the way storms loom in the distance as they creep closer and closer, and decide I am going to go with that notion a little more:

> Resounding in the distance
> Draws near and nearer still.

Resounding seems too gentle a word. I decide to cross it out and replace it with "roaring." Then I think more about the concept of roaring, like the way lions roar, which then makes me think of growling:

> Deep rumbling, like a growl

I desperately want to rhyme this with howl, but I don't want to create a pure rhyming couplet here. So instead I opt for internal rhyme with the next line:

> With the howl of the wind

But this seems weak. "With" is a bit of a weak word, but the storm is being driven by the wind. So

I cross out "with" and replace it with "driven on." Then I think of the storm building:

As builds the storm more quick

But this, while it has a nice poetic inversion of "builds the storm" instead of "the storm builds," does not sit well with me. I cross out "more," since the comparative form of "quick" is "quicker," and replace it with "so." I think of what a building storm looks like, and how angry it seems:

Rage boils, clouds roil,
Burgeoning thick, as gales
Drive and drive the heavy storm

Notice the device of a near-perfect internal rhyme of "boils" and "roil," and see how the consonance of "boils" and "gales" span across the two lines. Then I use repetition with "drive and drive," much like my use of "near and nearer" several lines previous. I call back to the idea that the sky is heavy—another form of repetition:

When in a final stormy blast

I look at this and think that this time I'm using too much repetition. Variations of the word "storm" have become redundant. So I cross out "stormy" and think of something better. I go back to my word associations and choose "tempestuous," then move on:

> The sky is loosed.
> Raindrops plummet, hail pelts

Yet I realize that I don't like the continued imagery of the storm itself raging. This has been about the storm building, and so "The sky is loosed" is sufficient to conclude it; it is also a good, simple poetic "turn"—the sky has been burdened and now it is free. Besides, it has the added benefit of calling back to the first line of "The sky is heavy." So I cross out the line about raindrops and hail and decide to leave it at that, leaving me with this as my first draft:

The sky is heavy.
Black clouds billow,
Burdened with weight.
Lightning's wrath
In thunderclaps
Roaring in the distance
Draw near and nearer still.
Deep rumbling like a growl
Driven on the howl of the wind
As builds the storm so quick.
Rage boils, clouds roil,
Burgeoning thick, as gales
Drive and drive the heavy storm,
When in the final tempestuous blast
The sky is loosed.

Now I just need a title for the poem. I love the first line so much, because it is both poetic and reminds me of my mother, so I decide to make that the title as well.

Step 5: Revision

At last, the poem is finished! Well, it's not really finished. Not yet. I still need to revise it. If I had chosen to write in meter, I would need to scan the verse carefully, count out the syllables, and pay attention to syllabic emphasis. I would need to be sure that all the stressed syllables fall in the right places. If it was rhymed, I would make sure I am really happy with my rhymes and not simply choosing a word for no other merit than, "it rhymes." If I decide I don't like a word I at first thought I loved, I'll cut it and replace it with something else. Then I must be sure that the meaning of the poem is clear (at least to me). If it rambles on and on, I will consider cutting some parts of it to make it more condensed and less wordy. I will also look for grammatical issues, because I have decided I want grammar to be a component of this poem.

As I look over my storm poem, I realize there are a few things that stand out as weak to me. "Deep rumbling like a growl / Driven on the howl of the wind" seems weak and not concise. So I revise it to:

Deep rumbling growls
Driven by howling wind

This is better, but I have lost the pure internal rhyme between "growl" and "howl," which I really liked. So I try again:

Deep rumbling growls
Driven by howls of wind

I am now satisfied. I move on to the next place that bothers me, which is "As builds the storm so quick." Something about this line just feels weak and unsatisfactory. So I consider a few options:

As fast builds the storm

But then I lose the repetition of sounds with "thick" two lines down. So I change it to:

As quick builds the storm

This is when I notice I use the word "storm" twice, which is not an effective repetition. At least, it doesn't seem effective. So I decide to leave this one and revise the phrase "Drive and drive the heavy storm." I have already done one call-back to "The sky is heavy," and I do it again in the final line, so that one has to go. So what do I use instead of storm? Clouds, perhaps? No, I have already said "clouds roil," and this is a repetition that would be ineffective also. What if I change the grammatical structure so I can replace "storm" with "them," where "them" refers to the roiling clouds? That would be perfect. But it loses some of its punch. So I ramp up the effective repetition. "Drive and drive the heavy storm" becomes:

Drive and drive and drive them.

I also don't like "When in a final tempestuous blast" due to its beginning word of "when." I can easily cut that. So I do. Then I notice an extra comma after "burgeoning thick," so I cut that. I am now left with this revised version:

"The Sky is Heavy"
by A.L.S. Vossler

The sky is heavy.
Black clouds billow,
Burdened with weight.
Lightning's wrath
In thunderclaps
Roaring in the distance
Draw near and nearer still,
Deep rumbling growls
Driven by howls of wind
As quick builds the storm.
Rage boils, clouds roil,
Burgeoning thick as gales
Drive and drive and drive them.
In a final tempestuous blast,
The sky is loosed.

Now, I will probably continue to pick at this for hours or weeks more, but you get the idea of the process. Revising poetry is a lot like revising prose, except that you are on the lookout for different types of problems. Once you are satisfied with your poem—or at least satisfied enough—share it with somebody else for feedback (if you're feeling brave) or tuck it away in a folder somewhere (if you're not). Once you have a second opinion, consider publishing it. There are a variety of poetry markets available.

Is it Really that Easy?

Can writing poetry really be as easy as only five steps? Yes, but it can also be as difficult as only five steps. Choosing a topic can be troublesome, which is why many people only write poetry when inspiration strikes them. Sometimes, word associations will escape you. Selecting a structure can be another difficult choice, and sometimes your structure will change halfway through writing the poem, leading to a more arduous revision process later on. Crafting the poem can take anywhere from minutes to hours. Revision can take months of nit-picking your poem into perfection. I have written poems which took me half an hour to write, and I have written poems where the crafting part alone took weeks to complete, let alone revision. I have dozens of unfinished poems, sitting on my hard drive patiently waiting for me to come back to them. You may discover after writing a few poems that my five-step process is not the process that works for you, and you will develop your own. It is my hope, however, that this will be enough to embolden you to write your own poetry with confidence until you find what works best for you.

Chapter Seven: When Words Collide

Conclusion

"Poetry is prose bewitched." —Mina Loy

Poetry is an art form all its own. Hopefully, this book has shown you that while prose and poetry are completely different, you can write poetry if you can write prose. The poetic devices of structure, sound, word choice and placement, repetition, metaphor, imagery, the "turn," grammar, and shape will help you as you strive to become a poet. Let your imagination run free and use as many or as few of them as you see fit while you let the words flow from your pen and collide on the page. The most beautiful part of poetry is that there is no wrong way to write poetry; there are less effective ways to do it, but there is no "wrong" way to do it.

Let that thought set you free as you embark on your poetry-writing journey.

Beautiful Collisions

For Further Reading

To help you understand poetry writing a little better, I highly recommend that you read in full those poems which I have cited in this book:

Goblin Market—Christina Rossetti

The Second Coming—W.B. Yeats

Those Winter Sundays—Robert Hayden

A Mongoloid Child Handling Shells on the Beach—
    Richard Snyder

The Highwayman—Alfred Noyes

Sonnet 130—William Shakespeare

Anyone Lived in a Pretty How Town—E.E. Cummings

Easter Wings—George Herbert (cited in full; I recommend you find an image of the original using your favorite search engine)

www.ingramcontent.com/pod-product-compliance
Lightning Source LLC
Chambersburg PA
CBHW071831020426
42331CB00007B/1689